Amor Aeternus

LOGAN
WALKER

AMOR AETERNUS
COPYRIGHT © 2019 BY LOGAN WALKER

All rights reserved. No part of this publication may be reproduced, distributed or transmitted in any form or by any means, including photocopying, recording, or other electronic or mechanical methods, without the prior written permission of the publisher, except in the case of brief quotations embodied in the critical reviews of certain other noncommercial uses permitted by copyright law.

Printed in the United States of America
ISBN: 978-1693909283

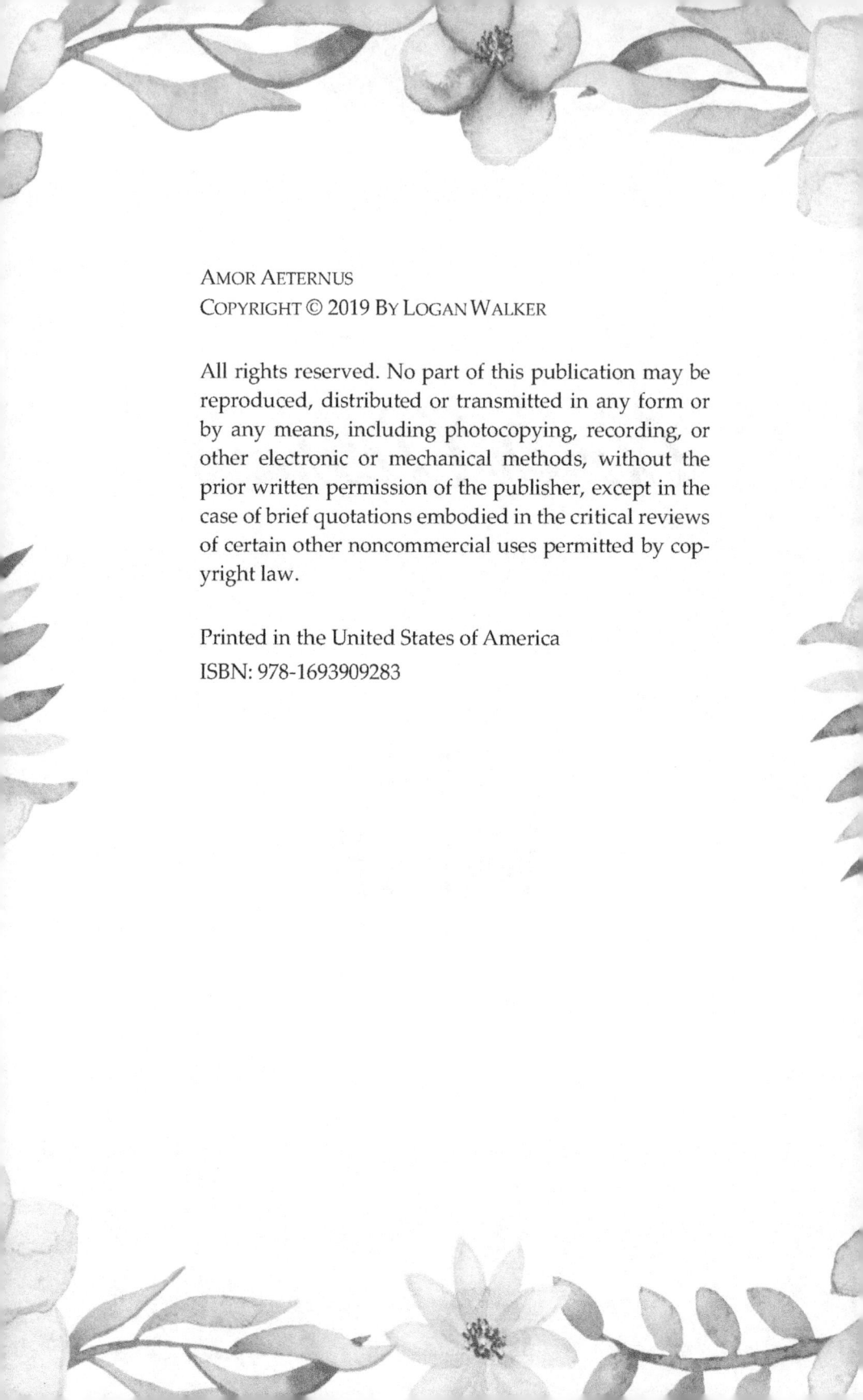

Dedication

To the woman who has always held my heart true, it has been nothing short of a pleasure and such a phenomenal honor to not only have known you but to have loved you and watched you grow into the woman you are today. Cheers to our continued adventures, the memories we've yet made, the hearts we'll touch with these poems, and to you for making me the luckiest man alive.

1

There has always been something special about you
That for the longest I couldn't just reach out and grab,
So I left the answer to what you mean to me blank,
The greatest mystery and the world's biggest case gone ice cold.

We know the obvious is "I love you," for I made it really clear to the world,
Yet the motive behind it forever changes, so they locked me away.

After almost a decade of letting my thoughts investigate everything in my mind,
I now have one last confession to make to the world—
The greatest crime, if one could call it that—
For my motives are anything but wrong.

In fact, my motives for loving you are the most sincere truths my heart buried.
Let it be known that I do, in fact, love you for many reasons.

I love the way your smile brightens not only my day—
It lifts the spirits of everyone in this world.
What's more is that I love the passion you have not only for music
But for those you hold dearest to your heart and your own beliefs.

I love both your sense of freedom and your stylish personality.
Not only do I adore how independent you are, but I respect it as well.

Hands down, I love the way you never leave my mind alone and
How the simple things we do send my heart to the heavens.

And to be honest, I don't know anyone else who makes me feel this way.
I feel as though, in any lifetime, we'd find one another as friends
Or possibly something greater than the closest of friends.

Whatever the case, I love you greatly, dearly, passionately, and deeply,
And now I truly understand the reasons why, after so long.

As for telling it to the world, if you were to look from my perspective,
You'd find I've done just that, for you are far more than just my close friend—
You are my sunny days when the skies are upset and rain dives from the clouds.

You are the calmest of seas in the midst of a raging storm,
Protecting and guiding me to the safety upon the shoreline.
You are the most peaceful and beautiful of forests,
Full of life and memories eager to be created.

Not to sound like I'm idolizing you, but you are my world,
And I guess after all these years and the months of deep-sea thinking,
I've come to realize that if I could have anyone to spend my life with,
I don't want anyone I just met or might've dated once or twice,
For their trust will never be completely there, nor will my heart be truly satisfied.

I'd choose the one who not only is my lover but my closest of best friends,
The one who'd stand up to me when I've done wrong by them
And would love me undoubtedly just for being myself.

If I had my choice of anyone in the world, I wouldn't have to think twice,
For my heart has known all along that it would be you.
I've wanted your happiness then, and that's all I want now.

2

With a soft smile to awaken nature for the new morning,
She opens her eyes to paint the clearest of blue skies.

From a distance, he watches in awe, trying to find the words,
For he is one of few words, and every time she's even close to him,
He freezes and listens as his heart runs up to the back of his mind,
Trying desperately to keep his thoughts from fleeing.

But it's not her beauty that causes the butterflies to race about his stomach;
It is the way she carries herself and the halo residing above her soul—
Representing everything that defines her personality and who she is as a person—
That makes a shiver run crazy up his spine.

Yet he can't possibly tell her that, for the word "amazing" is too simple,
And no other word seems to bring justice to coming close to describing her.

So there he sits, thinking of how to speak the unknown with a frown,
For even if the words had discovered his lost mind and come to save him,
He would only have his courage flee him the moment she came near him.

So he just watches the woman in awe from a distance
Whose smile awakens nature's blessings and whose eyes paint the clearest blue skies
For birds to fly high in and the world to enjoy.

3

So as I sit here thinking back to the beginning,
I see in the pond us in the library laughing and talking quietly,
Careful to not tip-off the librarian as to the motives of our conversation.

I lose all of my words as my thoughts come to a screeching halt,
As I stare in absolute awe into your forest-green eyes.

I see us walking the forest paths hand in hand, ready to take on anything and all,
And as your hand touches mine, I feel the spark ignited while it travels up my spine,
Setting my heart ablaze and leaving my heart burning brightly and eternally.

I can't possibly put into words just how much I love you so,
For even if there was such a way, it'd be lost deep within the swarm of butterflies
Awakened by our simplest embrace.

I have no clue what the future holds in store for us, nor do I care,
For as long as you won't let go, I'll keep holding on forever.
With a smile and a soft sigh, I gladly accept the task of telling the world I love you.

4

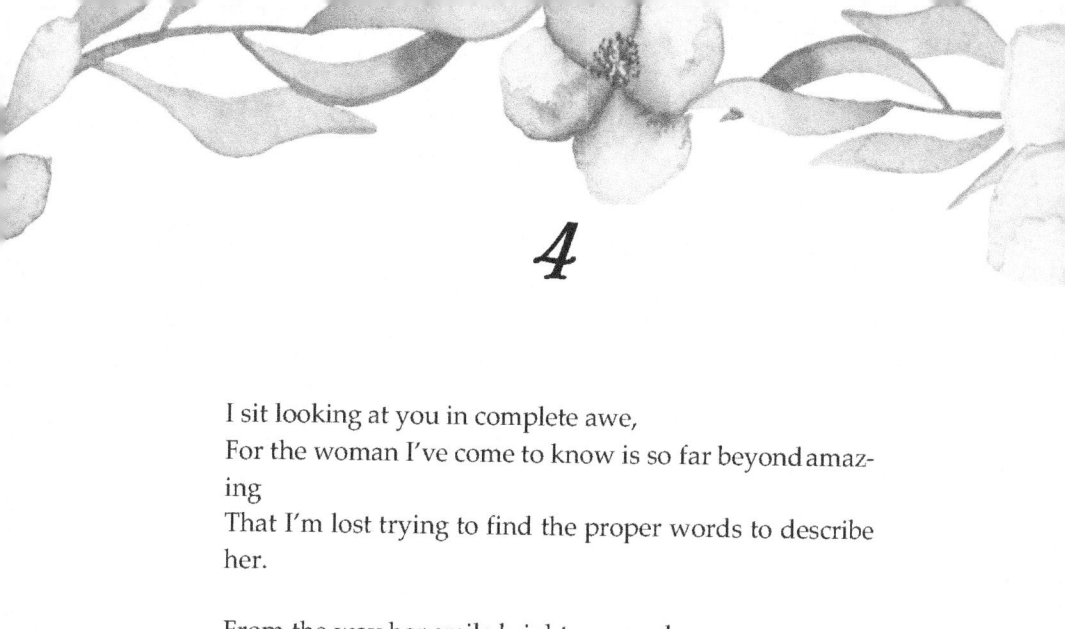

I sit looking at you in complete awe,
For the woman I've come to know is so far beyond amazing
That I'm lost trying to find the proper words to describe her.

From the way her smile brightens my day
To the comfort I feel simply talking to her,
Nothing could've prepared me for how truly blessed I've been
Having met and gotten to know one like her.

She claims to have flaws, and if she does, I don't care,
For I accept them and cherish her for who she is naturally.
Shaking my head, I see my thoughts clear enough.

With a subtle smile, I take your hands in mine
And make a promise (with your permission)
To not just be your boyfriend, but to be your man forever more,
Until time itself has ended its lifetime or until you no longer wish me to be,
Finding new ways to make you smile to brighten my world
And making my day the absolute best it can be.

I promise to be there for you through it all and to support you to my best,
And as I let go of your hands, please take the key to my heart.
Your kingdom there will be waiting to receive you with open arms.

5

He turns on the radio as the city lights fade into the horizon
And the stars begin to gather by the masses
While, subconsciously, he hums along to the songs of the radio,
Each lyric a different thought of her and every verse a new feeling.

Taking a quick glance at her smiling face, he felt at ease
As his soul joined its brethren in the sky above.
The moon is at peace, and nature has blessed the couple.
Turning the corner, they reached their destination:
A small hilltop overlooking the city below.

Turning the engine off, he steps out into the curtain of silver lighting,
And, with a deep breath, he turns and reaches for her hand,
Feeling his heart go racing off into the night with her slightest touch.

Pulling her closer, he notices they begin dancing not to the music that was playing earlier
But to the rhythm of their emotions and the harmony from the passion they share.

He soon finds that his smile hasn't faded since their journey began.
In fact, he smiles so much so that she asks, "Why?"
And, as he looks to his friends in the sky, he whispers,
"With everyone watching, I found peace here with you,
And I know that, now and forever, I love you."

6

He watches the moving stars as he collects his thoughts,
For there is someone new who asks to enter the city of his heart.
He trusts the idea and finds more reason to want her,
To open his gates.

The mystery of the unknown—to him, a question no longer,
For within her eyes, he sees all he needs and more.
And as they walk, hand in hand, through the maze-like streets of life,
He finds a friend, a lover, direction, a partner against the world.

And as dawn breaks through the morning sky and the sun awakens,
He believes from the depths of his soul that she can be the guardian of his
heart.

7

Take the hands and turn back time.
What lessons will be learned from the past?
Will you find the faults laying within my stars?

Listen to the rhythm of the calming wind
As we fall further into the subconscious abyss,
Gliding past the invincible barricade protecting my heart.

If only I knew the answer to the real question
Hidden behind locked doors with missing keys.
I want to know how to truly surrender my heart
So that I may become a better man.

Then maybe I could save us from this endless fall.
I ask you kindly, and I ask you sincerely
To take the hands and turn back time
In order to teach me how to love.

8

He punches the wall in disbelief, sending his pen flying across the empty room.
With a dramatic sigh, he takes a seat and begins thinking back to the day
That changed the path of his life in several unexpected ways—
From his writing to his perspective and outlooks. Even his morals changed then.

No matter how much time has passed, he still draws inspiration from where it began—
Living with the blessed curse of the feelings nature had given him.

He wonders if the person behind the curtain of his inspiration and affection even knows
The fact that they still inspire and influence his scripted pieces of art,
Or that the feelings he had then are the same ones coursing through his veins now,
Filling him with this invincible energy to take on and conquer the world.

Staring at the empty fireplace, he watches as their shared memories
Slowly fade into the small black rectangle.

Unable to do anything else, he smiles when the image of her smiling face appears,
For it was her smile that pierced his heart in the beginning
And stayed in his mind through their journeys in time.

Even now, her smile appears every now and then
Whenever he really needs it or just as subtle reminder to simply smile.
Moments pass as a tear quietly walks down his cheek to the ground below.

The memories fade away as he closes his eyes,
Turning his head towards the familiar sound of rain.
He listens in silence to the rhythm of her heart, and
Although they may never be together again, he knows they'll never be apart either.

9

Say yes!
Say yes to the opportunity of a lifetime
Where, through sunny and rainy days,
There will be someone there beside you,
Singing along or holding an umbrella
To shield you from the rain
Or to share a laugh while you dance
The day's tune in sheer bliss.

Say yes to that of the silent dream,
Giving it a chance to become reality,
Making people across the world happy
As the dreamer goes above and beyond
To remain within the dream
They sought for so long to be true.

Say yes to the genuinely appreciative
Whose selfless kindness had helped
Through many hardships and a road
Traveled too far alone in life.
It is they who will never steer you astray,
For they care sincerely about you
As well as your happiness and well-being.

I speak now for those in love
But don't have the voice to approach
The object of their deepest affections
Or struggle fighting for a chance
To shine in their hearts,
For I am one of those people.

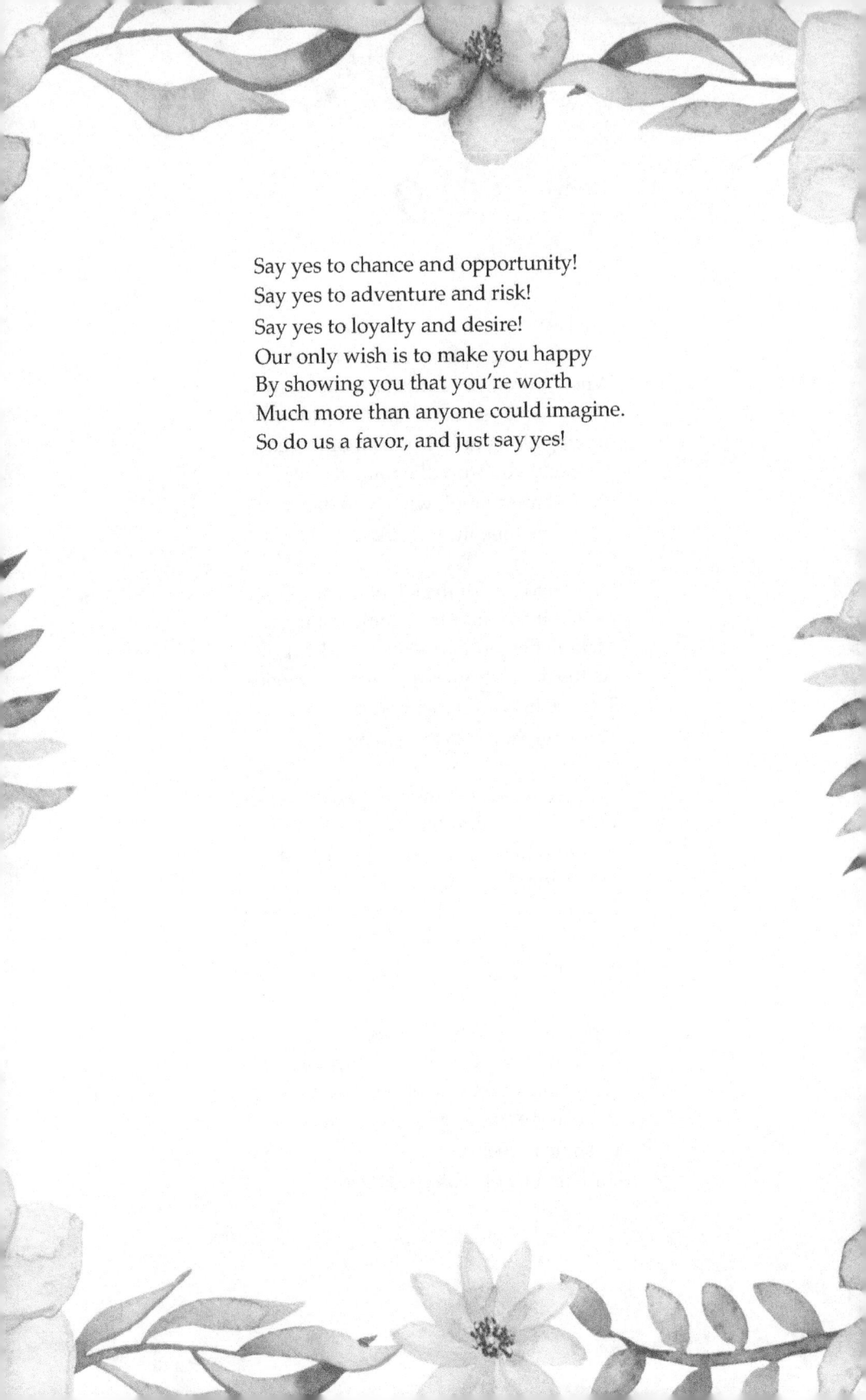

Say yes to chance and opportunity!
Say yes to adventure and risk!
Say yes to loyalty and desire!
Our only wish is to make you happy
By showing you that you're worth
Much more than anyone could imagine.
So do us a favor, and just say yes!

10

With everyone gathered around this warm campfire,
I think it's finally time to tell the truth and, for once,
Be honest with myself, my mind, and my heart.

'Tis been a long time coming since I've given an accurate account
Of the feelings I keep locked far away in the darker parts of my mind,
For they bring out the side most aren't supposed to ever see,
Exposing me to the mercy of the unnecessarily cruel world.

And though they introduce me to nature's curse—
To dance with the butterflies manifesting within my gut—
They also introduce me to the true and purely innocent beauty as well.

From the birds singing the comforting morning song
To the rain rhythmically calling any and all willing to come play,
I enjoy the finer things in life more so now than ever
Because I remember the lessons you've taught me.

And it's humorously ironic that I've never imagined myself
Genuinely feeling so special about someone
Who I've held dear to my heart for many years.

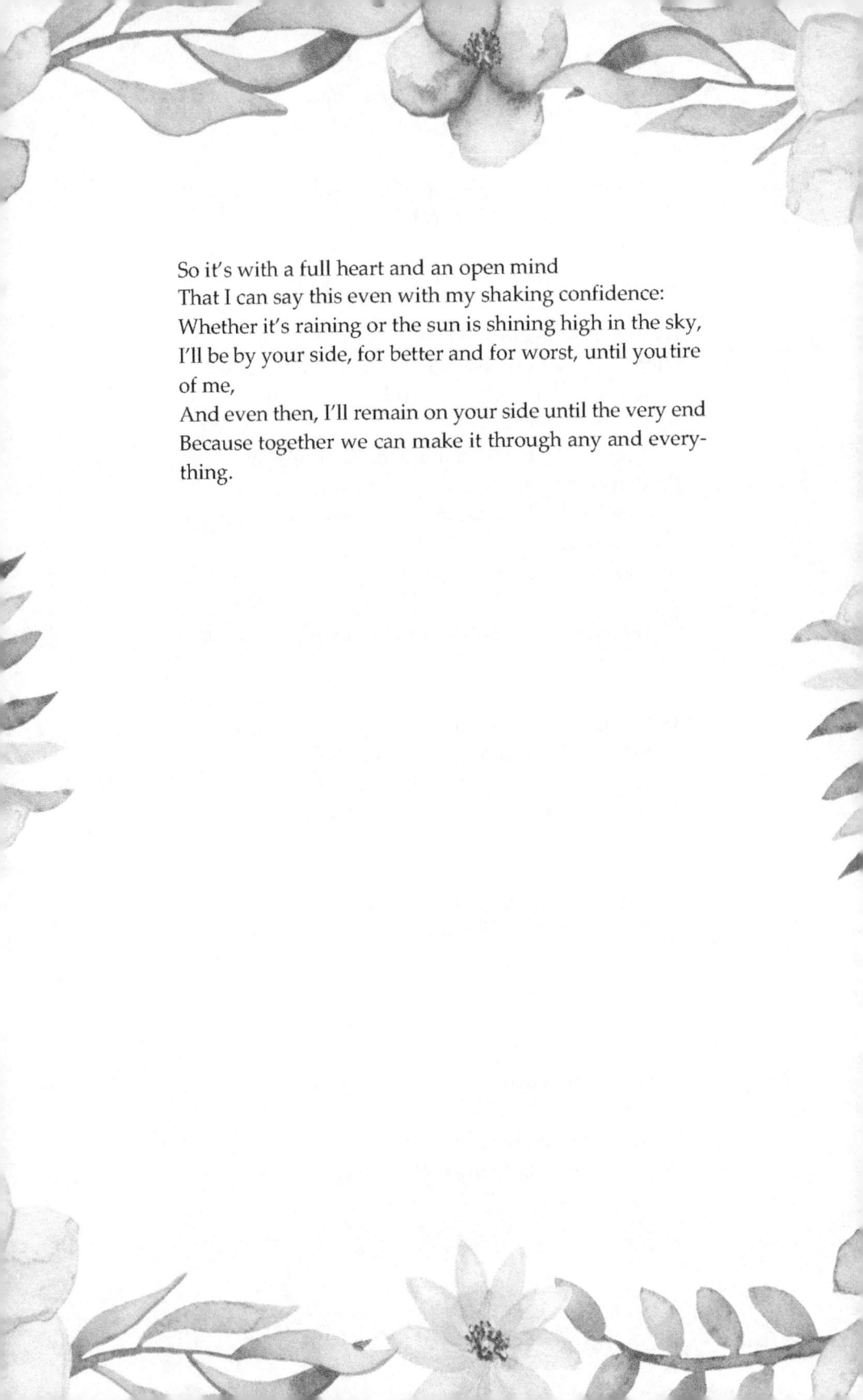

So it's with a full heart and an open mind
That I can say this even with my shaking confidence:
Whether it's raining or the sun is shining high in the sky,
I'll be by your side, for better and for worst, until you tire of me,
And even then, I'll remain on your side until the very end
Because together we can make it through any and everything.

11

Might I be honest with you?
You are the girl I want to fall in love with,
But I'm too nervous to say it, or I find myself
Second-guessing whether I'm your type.
As the wind, I'm often unnoticed as a gentle breeze
On the clearest of days when you shine the brightest.
To me, you're more than good enough for anyone.

Everything about you is what makes you unique and unlike anyone else,
And there is nothing I would change.
In that same sense, though I don't know much about you personally,
I do know that you're much more than just a one-night stand.

It's not even about the answers to the strangest things man can ask
But about the journey we could potentially have together.

I'm not one to control you, for that's never been my style.
I've come to appreciate you as a friend
Though I have hopes of one day being more.
From what I've come to know of you, I can tell
That you're a treasure worth more than
Any of these words I can put together.

12

I'll leave a note with the pen from my lips,
For it is much too hard to say face to face,
And I'd hate to disturb your peaceful slumber,
But to be honest, I have a confession to make,
And if I hold it anymore, surely I'll go mad.

I've loved you since the moment we met,
As innocent teens who didn't know much else,
To the time you said yes and set my world ablaze,
Burning brighter with the fuel from my dreams.

I've loved you through the good times
When our hearts danced countless nights away,
And through the bad times as well,
When our souls were at the other's throat.
A key to my heart will always have your name
Printed on it as a sign it's still yours to have.

I'll love you for the better moments
When we're the reason behind our smiles,
And for the horrid moments too,
When we can barely stomach looking at one another.

In fact, I will always love you to my heart's content.
It is because of that unyielding love that refuses to die
That I'm letting you go now
To pursue your happiness and to follow your heart.

13

He thinks of what to say as he taps the window,
For there isn't much he has not confessed
To the careless whispers lying anxiously in the wind.
With a deep breath, he listens to the calming rhythm
Of the fluttering drumbeat in his chest.

Taking a moment, he looks out to the flashback
When it all began, in the second floor of the restaurant.
With such a childish introduction, he couldn't help but chuckle
At the unlikely couple on the transparent screen.

Little did he know back then that the woman sitting down
Would become such an important part of his life,
Restoring hope in beliefs he thought drowned in his past's despair.

Giving a sigh of contentment, he knew the one thing he hadn't said,
As if his heart had hidden away this secretive song until it felt the time was right.

And now, with the approach of a new dawn,
He feels the energy of his heart screaming in a mischievous glee,
For now it wants nothing more than to shout this secret to the masses,
To wake the world with the harmony of the morning birds
Trying to settle the passionate inferno this secret has created in his heart.

He takes another breath to gather all the matching thoughts from his mind,
And, continuing the taps on the window, he begins the secret in perfect rhythm
Of the true feelings about her that he hid from the careless whispers
Lying anxiously in the wind for all those years.

14

Murder was what she wrote on my heart
Before stealing my breath away with a kiss.
I was unprepared for the surge of emotions
Spreading quickly through my veins.

My body starts to freeze as if they were liquid nitrogen,
And before I know it, I'm falling,
Not towards the ground but towards her.
With not a single ounce of strength to fight,
My descent into her is swift and hard.

For now I am sprung and in a mist,
Hopelessly confused, chasing after this feeling.
I can hear the birds singing as my heart beats faster.
Oh, such a lovely sound in a bad series of events!

Everything begins to spin the warmer my chest gets.
What is this sensation taking over me?
I see her silhouette in the distance,
And with my last ounce of strength, I run towards it,
Hoping that she can save me from this unknown adventure.

Instead, it vanishes as I'm seconds away from reaching it.
My vision starts to fade as I hear the sound of her laughter,
For murder was what she wrote on my heart
With the ink from the arrow she shot through my chest.

15

Excuse me, miss, could you please wait up?
For I'd like to give you this penny
So you can pay to listen to my thoughts.

Now, I know this sounds conceited,
And ordinarily I'd have taken the politer approach,
But for a special reason I stand
Before you now with a kind smile and an envelope
Holding the sincerest depth of my feelings.

I couldn't tell you how many voices gathered within my mind,
All with various reasons of why I feel this way,
Anxiously waiting their turn to strike the drum on my heart.

From the way your smile brightens my day
And awakens the creatures whose wings flutter,
Letting them dance as they please within my stomach,
To the way you're genuinely and simply you,
I wouldn't change you or any of your "flaws."

So when the day comes and love calls your name,
I hope to be the one standing outside the door,
Waiting for you to open your heart to me.

16

To be honest……
I sit picking the petals off of a rose, listing
All the reasons I can possibly make you smile—
From something no bigger than a house mouse
To something larger than the Empire State building.

I wouldn't mind making you breakfast in bed,
Served with a handwritten card and a simple tulip,
Or finding a new way of saying, "Good morning, beautiful."

I'd love to be there to watch you achieve your wildest dreams,
And, standing by your side on the front lines,
When the world seems to turn its back to you,
I wouldn't mind dancing the night away
Or gaming online until the sun breaks through the sky.

I suppose you could call me crazy for not knowing
The real reason why I'm willing to do all this and more.
An argument could be made that my feelings are showing,
But my rebuttal could be I simply love your smile—
An interesting debate for spectators to watch and listen in on
As I pull away the last petal from this stem.

There are dozens of roses within the world,
And with those, millions of ways to make you smile.
Finding them is a worthwhile adventure,
But for a moment, I just had to be honest.

17

Our spirits met by chance in a conversation
Months prior over simple pleasantries.
We laughed as they sang and danced,
Then we agreed upon a much-anticipated meet.

Little did I know that, in the moment our eyes met,
Everything within my world would combust into flames of change.
Photos that were already outspoken by your personality
Had no chance of redemption upon seeing you in person.

And there I stood for a silent few moments,
My legs fused with the freshly lain cement
As I tried to find words in the endless lists
Of the perfect things to say in times like this.

I felt the blizzard within my gut intensify
As my nerves began to falter.
Shortly thereafter, I felt something rather warm
Trickling its way down my chest,
Soaking my shirt in the process.

Looking down to find the source, all I could say was, "Damn…"
For in the midst of my internal chaos,
I never saw the bow drawn or the arrow placed dead center.

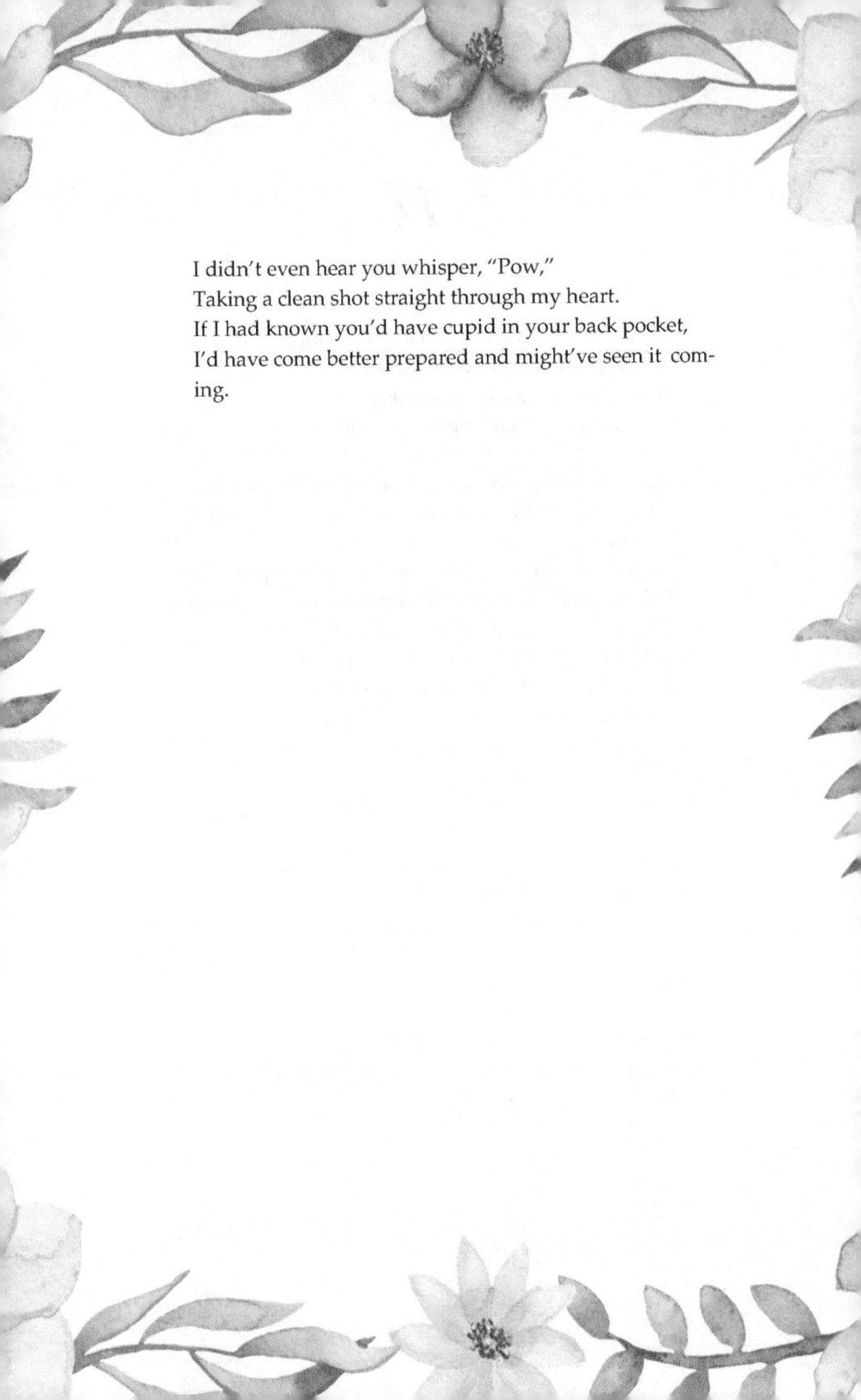

I didn't even hear you whisper, "Pow,"
Taking a clean shot straight through my heart.
If I had known you'd have cupid in your back pocket,
I'd have come better prepared and might've seen it coming.

18

I think of you more than there are stars in the sky,
And every time, I feel myself become one with the cement,
Awestruck and frozen in time's playground
Or lost in a hidden galaxy of far-fetched dreams.

I think about everything and anything relative to you,
From your smile to the sound of your laugh,
And the many ways to keep them around.
I think about the things you dislike
As well the instant detonators of your wrath.

I think about your hopes and your dreams,
Curious to see if I can help you reach them.
I think about your beauty and grace.
Oh, how I wish you only saw what I see!
Then you'd know why I think it so.

I think back to the day we met in the online media
To when we met in person in the busiest city imaginable.
There's not much that saddens me when thinking of you,
For I generally have better days in doing so.

However, one small thing brings tears to my heart,
And that's the idea that you're someone
Who's so genuinely amazing, and yet
You've accepted the idea that you'll be alone forever.
It saddens me to know that men in today's world
Have yet to realize just how much of a treasure you are.

Please do forgive me if I forget something here and there,
And please forgive me, for I may have said too much,
But this is what lies on the surface of my mind
When I think of you.

19

Here I sit in the blissful meadow between time and space,
Taken back by the subtle whisper of one specific name,
Carried through the breezes across the lands and over the water.

And I'm surrounded by the memories we've had up until now
While the fantasies and daydreams play on the puffy screens above,
Revealing the great adventure that has yet to be potentially written—
A heartfelt desire built upon the roads we've uncovered as friends.

Closing my eyes, I clear my mind and watch subconsciously
As the vastness of the morning sky expands beyond the horizon.

Yet within this silence, I can not only feel the rhythm of my heart,
But I can now hear the melody of the lyrics pouring out from my soul—
Quite the interesting song with a feeling of rejuvenation,
Something I had almost forgotten existed since being trapped
Within the deepest part of my own mental prison.

As this smile awakens on my face, my eyes open slowly,
Enlightened to what I almost took for granted,
And as if, by reflex, I reach down and grab a few flowers
To represent a symbol of not only you and me
But of the journey we could share in life.

20

Here within the shadows of love, I place a note
On the pillow next to your resting face.
Under the silver spotlight that broke through the curtains
From the crescent within the heavens, you look so peaceful.

Unfortunately, from this blissful sight I must digress,
For I have several heartfelt desires to confess.
If all it took for you to truly believe
That all I want is the reality of you and me
Was for me to tell the world that I will commit,
Then by the heavens, I'll gladly sign my heart and submit.

If only I could find my courage in the right place,
I'd be able to let my heart tell you to your face
Because I never expected to truly fall in love
Nor did I imagine that you'd be the one of which my heart sang.

We can relax now that my crime has been laid to rest.
As I hope for my sincerest dream to manifest,
I turn to whisper one last thing into the wind,
For soon this night will come to end.
I'll give you my heart, my soul, and my all
If you promise to never let our love fall.

21

I set the rose aside and quietly ask you, how can I say
That I've wanted to be with you from the very start
With nothing more than all the love in my heart.
Surely, with the sincerest of wishes, we can find a way
To do more than make our happiness drift day to day.

Wouldn't it be an absolutely crazy reality
If cupid's eulogy was meant for you and me?
Though I understand it may be hard for you to see,
Our hearts are desperately fighting to be free.

When we first met, I asked you to subconsciously believe in "we"
And entrust to me your heart's city key,
For I knew just how things would always be
Having time's good fortune to bless us eventually.

Most would say the justification for my feelings are based on vague superstition,
And, with a smile, I tell them it's a part of my creative intuition
Because it came to me in a very real dream-like premonition—
Or what religious people would scream to be a divine intervention.

I wrote your name on the back of the brightest star
And sent my wishes to the others off so far
Because I wanted any and everyone to know
That as time progresses, we will surely grow.

Now before you try to argue against this ironic prophecy,
Is it really so hard to see that it would happen eventually?

22

I thought for a while on all I had to say
To convince you that there was a way
For the love to return to us someday.
Then again, to be fair, I'll speak with nothing but honesty,
For that's always what you've given me.

I've had this dream that one day you and me would turn into "we,"
Creating the perfect symphony
Blessed with time's graceful harmony
And love's greatest melody,
Not eclipsed by the imagery of society
To become some faded and forgotten memory.

Now I must digress to confess that what you suggest
Is that you've kept my heart under arrest,
And I must attest to the fact that, in my mind, it's true,
Yet I'm lost on how to better express what you already knew.

With my pad and my pen,
I'll sit listening for your heart to say when
Of whether or not we can continue this chapter
In hopes of a random happily ever after.

23

As I lay back and prepare to dream,
On this silent night, all my heart wants to do is scream,
For most nights I lie awake with you on my mind,
Asking time if there's a way to pause and rewind.

Because no matter how I try to deny it,
From deep within my soul, I will admit
That I wish it was more than just a memory—
You and me against the world eternally.
So it's no surprise that when I close my eyes,
I see you in the distance, blocked by guarding lies.

The bridge between us is a serious work in progress,
Slowed by the memories I forcibly try to suppress.
And to be honest, sometimes all I can do is cry,
For even now, I stumble after simply saying, "Hi."

If I could ever muster the courage to tell you
About the feelings I hold to have always been true,
Maybe here in this fictional reality it could really be
That we could rewrite this eulogy with peaceful serenity.

But in the end, it's not my choice
To listen to or ignore the feelings after they've found a voice.
As I lay back and prepare to dream
On this silent night, all my heart wants to do is scream.

24

With everyone gone, I finally came to realize
That, in truth, I've been hiding behind written lies,
For it seems I spent this entirety speaking *about* you
Instead of directly *to* you on the feelings I hold genuine and true.

It never occurred to me honestly, you see,
That I creatively and unnecessarily made it what I felt it should be.
I didn't imagine that, at the time, hiding behind the intricate webs of fidelity,
Came a tainted energy that violated the sincerity of my integrity.

To be honest, it pained me more than you think to leave.
Hopefully, that is something your heart can believe,
For at the end of the day, you're more than just my muse,
You're the one out of everyone in the world I'll always choose.

To this day, I still find myself wondering why
Time has let the opportunity to be honest slip on by.
You were the one my heart could never shun,
And even against the odds, my mind refused to run.

As I sit on the dock under the silver moon,
I wonder if I'll know what's true soon
While I watch you sail away into the wrong bay
Instead of chancing it and coming my way.

Maybe it's wishful thinking to say I'd give you all my trust,
For my love is something sweeter than anything you would lust.
I swore that day to never leave you,
And if given the chance, I'd gladly prove it true.

25

Within the final moments of the sunset's fading smile,
I think of every reason to convince you to stay awhile,
For if this were the absolutely perfect dream,
Everything wouldn't be exactly as it seems.

'Tis true that I was the one to notice your pain,
Painted clearly across the canvasses glistening in the rain.
And yes, I realized that while into the darkness I was falling,
Your name alone was the one I continued calling.

Maybe there are a series of mysteries in the shadows who can relate
To how two soul-matched lovers could share such a bittersweet fate.
Then again, maybe I'm crazy to think fate will bless us with a date—
That our love would flourish, dominate, and recreate.

You have always been more than just my best friend,
Bringing forth many adventures I wish would never end.
Just promise that you'll indeed wait for me,
And I'll be the one to save you from this birdcage reality.

26

Over the years, several things have enlightened me,
Helping shape the world the way I envisioned it to be.
I used to always wonder the reason why
My heart fought so much just to try.

Was the answer hidden in your intoxicating smile
Or how you convinced a guy like me to stay awhile?
Maybe it was encrypted in the melody of your beautiful voice
With the message offering up a better choice.
Or could it have been your genuine sincerity
That brought my mind its peaceful clarity?

I don't think the answer is simply just one,
And I hope this makes sense when I'm done,
For it seems that the combination of my imagination and reality
Allowed you to also see through the mystery
Of love and Fate's profound philosophy.

Just the other day, I came to realize
That there are things I can't hide with lies.
I tried to fight and ignore the obvious sign,
But my heart was forever yours, not mine.

There are a lot of things I can't do over the phone,
And from deep within my soul, for my sins I will atone.
If by some fortune-blessed miracle, there's a chance,
Then I'll gladly give it everything in one last dance.

My thoughts begin to pace in my mind to the rhythm of a metronome,
Wondering if the day will come for you to come home.

27

The day we first met replays constantly in my mind,
And through time, my heart has become the beast in this rodeo.

But did anyone ever really stop and wonder why
I feel so passionately, so strongly about you,
Or why my soul decides to joyously dance with such a vibrant energy
Simply because you just so happen to be around?

Our relationship was so platonic; it was insanely adorable.
Though to be completely honest, that was absolutely fine by me,
For it allowed me the opportunity to explore the world in your mind.

It isn't because of how I felt the day we had our first kiss,
Even though I was entranced in a peaceful bliss
Days after it had come and gone.

Even in our most recent series of escalated adventures,
Though I still can't find the right words to describe
The state of my mind after all this time,
Is not the reason why I've held all these feelings deep inside.

It's because of the way you made me feel in those brief moments.
I was taken on an adventure, unlocking door after door
Of the many mental layers of defense put in place years prior.

There was one fantasy that stayed in my mind
After things had calmed and time blessed us with good memories.
Though with that blessing, the fantasy became warped
Into a simple and ironically impossible wish,
Sent religiously to different stars each night.

The real reason why I can never stop loving you
Is because no matter how much time passes,
Or how much life tries to throw our direction,
Everything feels right and so enviously free with you
That I had grown to want nothing more than for it to be true.

28

You know, most nights I sit up thinking of what to do.
Whenever you walk through the door and say, "I'm home,"
I could dim the lights and light a heart full of candles,
Welcoming you with freshly picked roses and a smile on my face,
Or I could have some of your favorite foods spread across a blanket
In front of the fireplace after a hard day's work.

I've thought about setting up a movie night for just us two,
Even something insanely just for fun out in town.
I'd paint the night sky with your wildest daytime fantasy.
Then again, I'm a terrible painter, so I may have to substitute that...

But I'm willing to give it my all in finding a new way to see you smile.
I know this is cheesy and rather childishly silly;
However, I have found myself deeply infatuated with your smile.

It makes me forget about my troubles for a tiny little bit—
My own personal escape from this insanity we call reality.
So I will do my best to always make you smile
Whenever you walk in the door and say, "I'm home."

29

Here by your side is where we will always choose to stand:
On one side as your best friend and, on the other, a sincere lover.

It is debatable amongst those who don't know
Whether we have the right to honestly have a place here
Or if one of us would willingly betray your heart's trust.
But to be honest, we'd burn the world down
Before we would ever let you fall.

If it ever came to be a question of our motives,
And we had to prove our heart's conviction with the truth,
It's not because of the private things that could occur behind closed doors
Or because we're looking for medals or some sort of gratification.

It's because we had a late-night realization after exploring our mind
That, even if we had to lose close to everything,
It'd be worth it if it meant we were able to save you.

Now, I've been speaking of "we" as if it were just you and me
Though in actuality, I was speaking of me in duality.
For not only am I standing tall as your best friend through it all,
But also as the sincere lover who'd give everything
To never let your happiness fade away and fall.

30

Boom...you can hear the gasp for air and the soft thud
As my vision blurs on my way to the ground.
I awaken hazily to the image of your face and am confused.

How did I end up on the ground, and where are we now?
More importantly, when did you get here and are the paramedics coming?

I try to lift my arm to feel the open wound.
Though unable to fight against your calming touch,
I lay there and let my vision fade away again to gray.
Internally, I can hear my heart beating normally,
So I relax a little, for no longer am I a dying man.

Searching for the location of the wound is hard
Because there's no entry point, no blood escaping.
Panic engulfs my mind as the confusion spreads,
And for the first time, I hear your voice softly in the back of my head.

It's calming and puts my soul in a trancelike rest.
Everything is quiet again, and my thoughts are gone.
Suddenly, the panic arises again at the acceleration of my heart,
And everything stirs into a massive, chaotic frenzy.

From the tiny openings in my eye lids, I see you bent over.
It is then that I notice my lips are warm and my cheeks damp.
Soon, I realize that not only were you crying,
But that you had leaned over to pour your heart into me with a kiss.

Slowly, the idea begins to manifest as my vision returns.
For once, I'm left speechless, trying to rationalize this feeling.
I see a small figure with tiny wings and a large bow.

Looking down, I can see an arrow slowly fading into the night—
The same kind of arrow fading from the same spot on your chest.
Then it hit me that we had become the pawns
In cupid's little game of finding love.

31

I remember the days when, here on this stage,
My biggest fear was performing for you, not the world,
Because I could perform with the façade I wore so well
With little to no care for anyone in the world.

Yet the day I met you, the mask was shattered,
And for the first time ever, the real me had been exposed.
Questions and doubts swarmed my mind, consuming it.

For that reason, doors were locked and things were left unsaid.
Soon, it became a monster I could no longer battle alone.

I gave into the fear caused by my own insecurities,
And I thought I took everything and fled behind the wall.
However, my heart stayed and continued to fight,
For it knew the potential we could've had in time.

It believed the sincerity of the "I love you's" that filled it with joy.
As time progressed, my writing grew into letters from my soul,
Left in tiny little envelopes waiting at your door.

Thinking back, I've always been able to make you smile.
Through similes and a clever use of word play,
Our minds danced long after the sun had gone to rest.

And with these metaphors tethered to my veins,
I created arrows aimed at the center of your chest
So that we could finally have a heart-to-heart conversation.
Long-overdue questions will finally meet their answers
As the world watches our story unfold.

There is something I would hope you already know:
That whether the answer is yes, no, or simply unknown,
My heart only recognizes home as anywhere with you.

32

As I walk along these empty streets, I find myself wondering:
If I kicked a stone hard enough, would it reach out to you?
Or if you hear my heart whenever it calls your name.

I can remember clearly the time when my heart froze,
When my soul had manifested beside me in awe,
When you looked my way the first time so long ago.
Regardless of whether or not the roads we took carried us apart,
Somehow, we always found a way to return to one another.

I used to think that I was never going to be good enough,
And still you chose to believe in the potential of me.
I can't apologize enough for not believing then
That you had the power to make my heart home.

And who's to say that if I turn a corner, I won't find you,
Standing with a genuine smile and open arms,
Still just as ready to make the fragile empty house
Your peaceful loving home in the city within my heart?

As I walk along these empty streets, I find myself wondering:
If I kicked a stone hard enough, would it reach out to you?
Or if you hear my heart whenever it calls your name.

33

Someone asked me the other day what love meant,
And, ironically, my voice caught itself because I thought of you.
My confidence faltered a bit at the sight of bittersweet memories,
But my heart held true to its conviction to be heard.

Love is the adrenaline that surges through your veins.
It's your name whispered in the wind.
It's the smile that rips through storms for the sun to shine.
It's what inspires my mind to motivate my soul to awaken for the day.
Heh, it's the reason I laugh; it's the reason I cry.

Love is an indecisive trickster looking for a place to belong,
And it's all too easy to find yourself lost in its eyes,
For in one you see the joyous memories that soothe your heart
Although in the other you see the knife that pierces your soul.

In fact, love is the reason it feels so good with you in my arms
And the culprit for why it hurts me whenever you say goodbye.
I know I say this often, but I hope you believe
That, sincerely and genuinely, I love you so.

34

To simply say, "You're amazing," is an understatement
That even the heavens we pray to would frown upon.
And I can't tell if the reason is hidden in the way you smile,
But I can say that it's what shines through on the darkest of days.

Or maybe the reason is hidden in the safety of your embrace
That helps put my restless mind in a peaceful bliss.
Could it be written on your face when you look at me
With such gentle eyes to see me for who I am?

There are many more ways that make you far beyond amazing,
From your kindness and honesty to your humble confidence,
Including everything that can't be described in words.

I know that I sound completely out of my mind for thinking so,
But I guess that's because, to the world, you've always been
Just another woman trying to make it on your own
Though to me, you've always been the world.

So unfortunately, I can't describe what would surpass amazing,
But I'm glad nonetheless that you are who you are.

35

It truly is the smallest things that mean the most to me,
But they also are the hardest to understand.
Maybe it's because I mull over things in the darker parts of my mind,
And the shadows that lie within tighten their grip on my heart.

What was in the message hidden in your smile
When I casually called you my baby while the song played?
Was it something you wouldn't mind or was it nothing more
Than cute, innocent humor between us in the scarce moments we have alone?

Why is it that we're extremely protective of each other,
And yet we do our best to shield the other from our own troubles?
Does it turn you on when I challenge your authority
Or when I say something randomly romantic from my heart?

As the days pass, the list of questions grows and the mystery continues.
And here I sit, thinking of the good and the bad
While still discovering new things about the life you've lived until now.

To this day, I still look at you and smile just as much as I did
The first day I met you almost a decade ago.

36

I sit resting my fingers gently on the piano glistening in moonlight,
And as the rain knocks quietly against the window,
I listen to the rhythm of your heart as my thoughts sort themselves.

With the first couple of notes, I watch the memories
Glide by on closed eyelids, and I'm lost in the adventure,
Traveling through the harmony of how we came to be.
The tempo quickens as my fingers begin to dance faster
Just to match the growing intensity of the drumming rain.

Fantasies stemming from various figments of my imagination
Paint the halls within my mind of what life could be
If only time had blessed us as "we" instead of you and me.

The melody takes control and slows the tempo down for a few seconds,
Giving my heart a chance to catch its breath before the bridge.

It's always struggled with the finale because of nerves.
Though words weren't enough, my thoughts scattered,
And a speechless me fled far away into the night.
But this time, I'm not afraid, for the song is almost at its end.

I open my eyes and feel the heat from the keys
As my fingers move furiously and swiftly into the final notes.
In the silence that follows, I feel peaceful yet anxious.

For as the invisible crowd begins to cheer, I pray
That the feelings I hold dear in my heart reached you—
Wherever you are in the world—and brought a smile to your face
The way you always bring one to mine.

37

Here I stand next to my heart on the frontlines,
Wearing the scars of your past as reminders that we've come so far—
Faded memories reflected across our backs from the horizon.

We can look into the distance at what the future holds—
Patches of falsified security mixed in with
The vengeful mysteries of the hurricane ahead.
Yet my worries aren't about what's ahead
Or even what may lay buried behind us.

I'm focused on the now and the pictures of the timelines
We've painted across the skylines.
I remember the times when you held me down.
You had the power then to always turn my day around.

You followed me down every road regardless
Of whether it was pleasant or not,
Fighting to see if, in the end, I truly loved you or not.
Were there many voices in your mind or a singular thought
That forcibly created such a shadow?

It eclipsed my heart's eternal meadow,
Pushing you away in your own blanket of fear,
Implying a dark end is, in fact, unfortunately near.
Can we have a moment of silence for the hearts about to be broken
When those final grave words are softly spoken?

With all your faithful and appreciated trust,
This next task is an absolute must—
Take a breath and relax your mind,
For now is the time to sit back and unwind.

If I'm to be open and completely honest,
Then it is true you deserve nothing short of the best,
And for the longest time in this current life,
I've had the dream of one day making you my wife.

38

Do you ever wonder where our hearts go
When our souls collide as they ascend
With the realization that I do love you so,
In hopes that, with time, our scars will mend?

You constantly inspire me to do better
As our love expands in and out of time.
I put my feelings in the signature of this letter
And hope that you'll stick around for one more rhyme.

Nothing is always smiles and happiness,
For you left in my heart broken daggers.
I beg that you end this madness
While, shocked, the fragile me staggers.

What does it truly mean to be in love?
Is it just figments of our imaginative minds—
Full of peaceful memories or lack thereof—
Or just a method to help us get lost in rewinds?

Honesty is and truly will be the best policy.
I hope you didn't get lost in the moonlight,
Trying your hardest to find your way back to me,
For I've departed from the world on this night.

Though I must digress with moments left,
I have one more thing I simply must confess:
This was never a crime of extraordinary theft,
For the longest my feelings I tried to suppress.

In the brightest lights and the shadows of the dark,
I'll always ask and request that, anew, we start
Because on us is that of the ancient mark
Left by those we cannot see in the shape of a heart.

39

For the longest, I've always considered you my baby,
And as a result, my rhythm was never blue
With the hopes that one day it would come to be
That the love in my heart you'll find to be true.

I know it scares you that I seem so surreal—
Too good to just be true for one like you
After years of enduring every possible ordeal—
Yet here I am, begging to start anew.

You've always been more than my best friend,
Standing constantly by my side throughout time.
I'll promise to be with you until the very end,
And I'll prove that loving you, in fact, isn't a crime.

The first time we met, I fell in love with your smile.
I knew I had to act quickly to make it last,
Then maybe I could convince you we'd last awhile
As I did my best to make amends for the errors of the past.

Though how I've felt has never been a mystery,
By my name I swear to always give my best.
I hope that I've impressed throughout history
And that we could leave out all the rest.

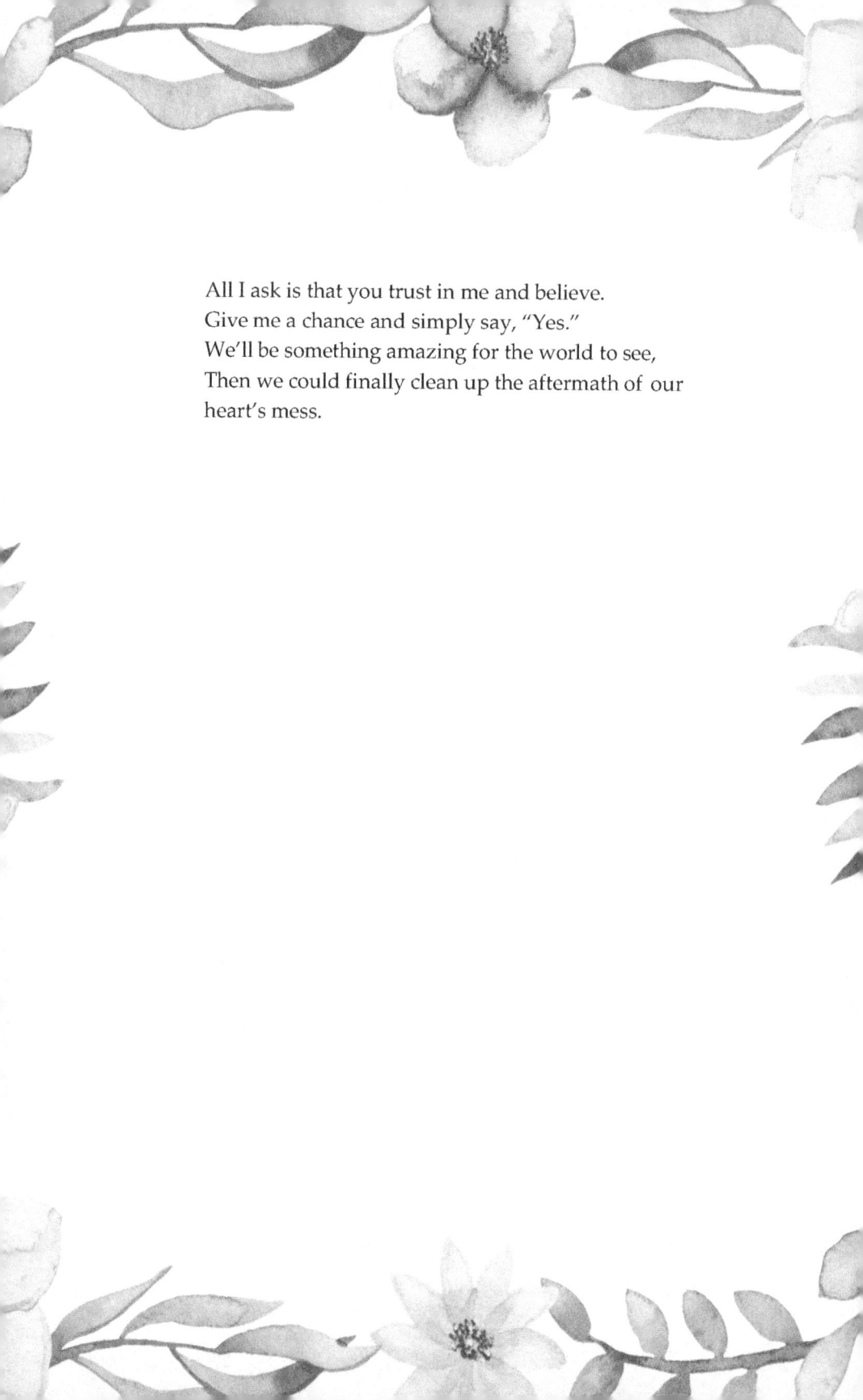

All I ask is that you trust in me and believe.
Give me a chance and simply say, "Yes."
We'll be something amazing for the world to see,
Then we could finally clean up the aftermath of our heart's mess.

40

It was when I first saw you smiling at me,
In a moment stopped perfectly by the hands of time,
I picked up my pen and began to write,
Noticing that my pen strokes fell in perfect rhythm
With the subtle and steady beat of my heart.

Together with that moment engraved in my mind,
I transcended to a different universe
Where my thoughts flowed along in streams of peaceful currents,
Traversing the lines of page after endless page.
It was then I truly fell in love with poetry.

Over the years, people have watched the debate
To see whether or not I had really fallen out of love.
Instead, as I grew and matured, I watched as it blossomed
Into someone more beautiful than I had words for.

And she seemed to capture everything in several verses,
Like the importance of her value in many clever metaphors
Or the ways I try to express my feelings in the amicable similes,
Realizing that I was lost deep within the eulogy.

For some, poetry is their best friend,
The ray of light in the dark chambers of the mind,
And for others, it's where they find freedom to escape the madness,
Express their inner most private feelings in an unusual way.

But for me, poetry is much more than just my muse—
It's my wings to fly and what keeps me grounded.
It's the silver lining to my ongoing mystery of life,
The fire in my eyes serving as the inspiration to always be better,
And the motivation to never give up when things get rough,
And it's funny because the day I fell in love with you
Was when I truly fell in love with poetry too.

41

I never knew it was possible to miss someone this much
Until I thought about how much I miss you—
From the way your hand feels in mine
To the small, perfect moments we create in and out of time.

I miss the way your smile warms my soul and touches my heart
As well as the unspoken feelings when I look into your eyes.
I miss the joys within our laughs along with the pain that never lasts,
And that's not even the best part.

Honestly, for me, the best part is that unexplainable feeling
That happens when I awake each morning, smiling
Because I know I'm not only in love but loved by
The amazing person I'm lucky to call my best friend.

I can't thank you enough for your patience
And for genuinely caring the way you do.
Words simply aren't enough to express how much I appreciate you,
So without further ado, this is my simple ode to you:

I don't have much to offer, and I know I'm cheesy,
But my best I'll give simply to make you smile,
For better or worse, with the bitter and the sweetness,
By your side, I'll always stay.

42

Is you is or is you ain't my baby?
See, most days I awake with a smile,
Considering myself the luckiest man in the world—
Not simply because I'm in love with a woman
Who's a true example of beauty at its absolute finest,
But because that same woman was kind enough to look my way.

You see, guys like me never win chances with women like her,
For with all my faults, I'm still considered a good guy.
So unfortunately, realities where she and I are "we"
Get lost in the world of infinite dreams.

Then of course, there are the days
When I'm just like, "Damn, can't even get a kiss good-bye!"
And by no means am I saying that I'm ungrateful,
For I really appreciate the morning texts and all you do.

I know you love me and care greatly as well
Though to this day still it baffles me.
However, I've learned not to question it
And just enjoy the time spent creating memories.

What's more is the irony when I'm told
People actually want what we have,
And as much as it makes me smile,
I'm just as baffled by the statements.

For I myself am unsure of what it is we have,
And to force your hand into something I want
Would go against who I am, and I know it would
Ultimately make you completely unhappy in the end.

Are we the undying love story of Romeo and Juliet,
Where our love keeps us alive instead of killing us?
Or are we the sad tale of the gods Geb and Nut,
Two lovers chosen by fate to never be together?

Or we could be the start of a new legend for generations to come?
Whatever our story is, I'll sit and wait until time is ready to tell.

43

If I bought you a single, freshly picked rose,
Would you call me from work just because,
Or even maybe tell me you love me
Just from the look in your soft, warm eyes?

Whenever you touch my hand, I get a shiver down my spine,
For the feelings in my heart turn the courage in my mind to ice.

And in the following moments, I'm completely frozen
As you pull the daggers out of the crawling time.
Can't a man have his own dreams
When things are never as they seem?

You're so sophisticated, and I'm highly educated, but that's all overrated.
I studied the way of philosophy so we could take off in astronomy.

We could talk theoretical bars while we dance amongst the stars.
I told you that I'd give you all my heart,
And I meant every word from the start.

If the stars aligned to allow me to grant you the world,
Then, by the variety of gods above, I would,
But here in this reality, I can only give you my all
In hopes that I could give the world metaphorically.
As the oceans wash away the sands of our past,
You are the only one in my mind who's first and last.

44

Would you believe me if I told you
That you make me feel like I can fly
Higher than any bird in the world—
Like the stars aligned themselves perfectly
To be the feathers of the wings I spread?

So it should be of no surprise to you
That when day comes and night falls,
It is your smile I wish to see
When I awaken in the morning light,
For as free as you make me feel,
It's also with you that I feel the safest.

From the countless times you've had my back
To the stubborn drive to prove that
You'll always be here no matter what's to come,
I truly wouldn't have kept my sanity if you hadn't
Pulled me back into reality whenever my mind wandered
Too far away to where it was lost in the clouds.

Y'know, the funny thing about everything is
The world has a twisted sense of humor,
For I was convinced that I could float
Straight through life being cold and content,
Breaking hearts as they come and watching
As those who believed exit out the door of my life.

That all changed, however, when I met you.
I began to believe in what most would call myth,
And as time progressed, I found peace of mind
Whenever I imagined your smile
Or the way we seemed to escape the world
When it was only just the two of us.

I'm also painstakingly aware of how my infamous
Cheesy, corny lines had become clichés,
But it's in the simple statements—replayed over
Countless times on the last of the spinning records—
That the truth finds its most sincere form.

You see, I love you because I need you—
Not to say that I am unable to take care of myself.
I need you because, as strong as I am,
There are some things in life I can't fight alone.

And there's also the fact that I want you
Because of the same reason back then
And even more so years from now.
It's not because I can't have you, but simply because
I couldn't make it without you.

45

To the mystery woman at the head of our class:
I couldn't help but notice the way you smile is contagious.
To say I'm not in the least bit curious would be a blatant lie,
For it's not just the beauty of your smile that entices me,
But the story hidden in your eyes caught my attention.

And the warm, comforting aura radiating from you
Was almost impossible to ignore—let alone resist—
But for a quiet guy like me, there aren't enough words
For me to accurately describe the way I see you
Or even all I'd love to know about the journey you've had so far,
Although I can scratch the surface by saying truthfully that
Your personality shines brighter amongst the stars.

And with a heart made from the purest of diamonds,
To simply say you're beautiful is an understatement.
But I must digress because I do have a question—more so a request:

Would you do me the honor of having the pleasure
Of sitting here for a while as you tell me the stories of your life
And the many ways to keep that smile on your face?

46

Who exactly do you think you are?
And what do you think gives you the right
To leave my head in the clouds, dazed joyfully,
To poison my veins with a certain adrenaline
That causes my heart to run wild,
Skipping a beat now and then in the chaos?

What makes you think it's okay
To steal my breath away with a kiss
Or to fill my mind with images and memories
So my thoughts are drowned in missing you?

Please tell me your justification
For the satisfaction you took in breaking into
The city guarded within my heart
When, for years, I built walls to keep people out?

Where do you get off storming into my castle
With an army under the claim to protect?
And now here you stand, trying to seduce me,
Promising to be everything I've ever wanted,
All I could dream of and more.

So I will ask you again for the last time:
Who do you think you are?
 "…I am love."

47

Do you remember?
There was a time where it used to be
Against the world stood you and me.
We would always laugh and rarely cry
On just how far my dreams could fly.

Surely you know I would have died
If ever came the day when you wouldn't ride.
You shot an arrow straight through my heart,
And I have loved you from the start.

I have been yours since day one—
My number one who sets and rises with the sun.
Time flies faster than planes in the sky.
You're so distant now, and I wanna know why.

In place of me, you built a stone wall—
Maybe as a sign for me to continue to fall.
Will this dance between us ever end?
Or by chance, can we save it and make amends?

The bond we built began to drop,
And time mercilessly refused to stop.
If true love really does exist,
Then why does your heart insist?

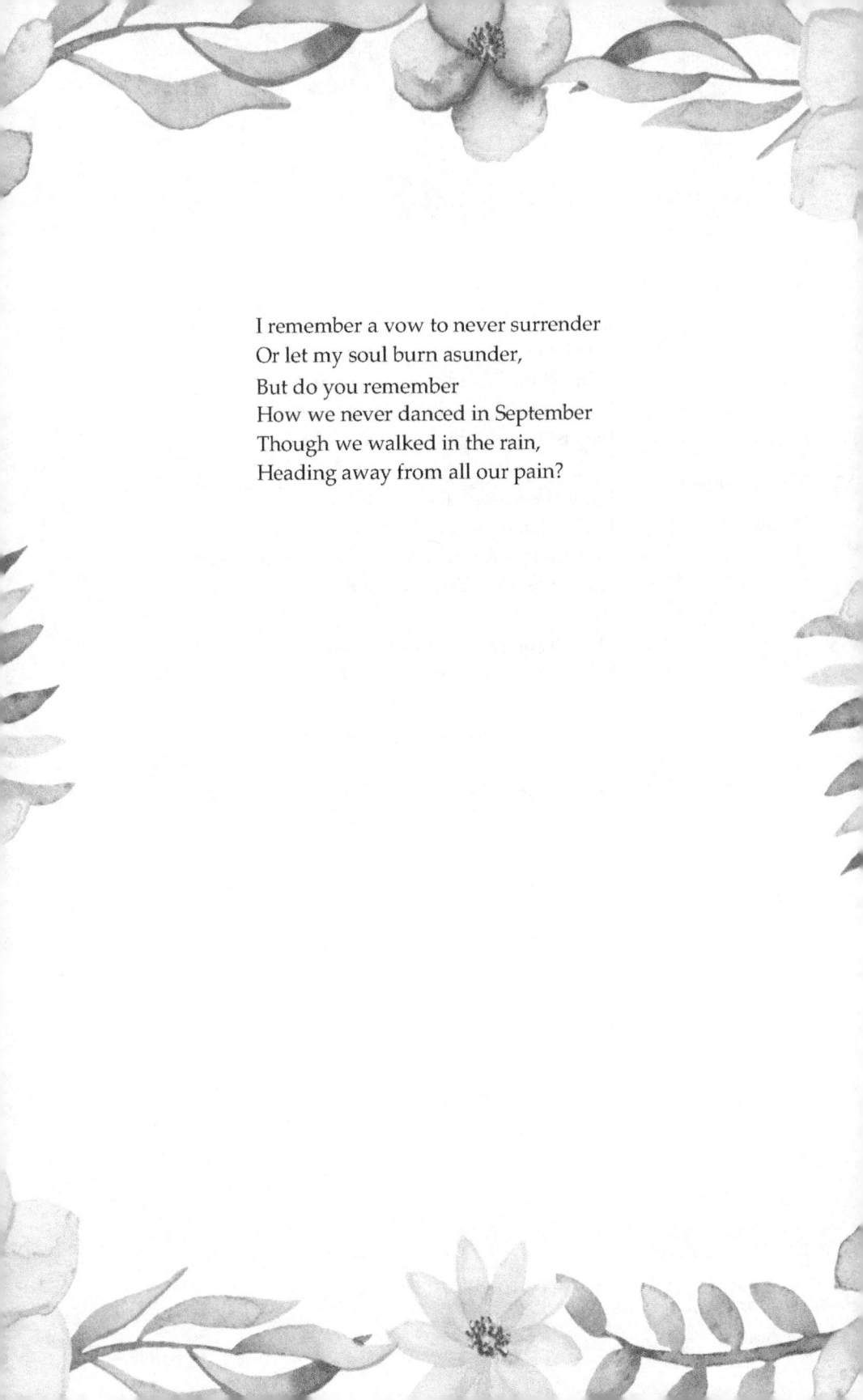

I remember a vow to never surrender
Or let my soul burn asunder,
But do you remember
How we never danced in September
Though we walked in the rain,
Heading away from all our pain?

48

I find myself stuck staring at my reflection,
Looking through a mirror with a single crack,
Which serves as the reminder of my imperfection.

And as my thoughts loudly continue to stack,
The question remains as clear as the day,
For there never was an answer to, "Why
Do you keep my heart so far away
Like you're waiting for me to cry?"

Can't you and I sit back and reminisce?
It's funny how much time will change,
Passing along, disrupting my peaceful bliss,
And yet you probably think I'm strange.

If love really is the mythical battlefield,
Then why send me out with a broken heart
To use and defend myself in place of a shield?
Such an unfair war that I lost from the start,
Even through all this chaotic madness.

I can't drown out the obnoxiously spiteful voices.
Hence, I am forever trapped in their sadness,
Feeding on how life will give you better choices.
Why did I ever take a chance and stand on the front line?
And why did I ever think you were truly ever mine?

49

There are countless beautiful women
Sought throughout the world daily,
And yet, in spite of that, I've always simply
Searched only for you.

If it were possible to grab the hands of time,
I'd stop them every now and then
Just so I could admire your perfection
In a timeless moment that will be cherished.
Because I've seen the way you walk
Through a crowded room, capturing gazes,
Making their heads turn with locked awe.

And believe it or not, I've actually listened
To the words you preach to grow stronger—
The phrases and speeches meant to push us
As well as the humbling responses to those
Who see the reason to feed your ego.

There was a time when I told you that
You were the woman of my dreams
Because it terrified me to my core.
Now I will tell you that you will always be
The woman in my dreams during the day
And even the ones in the night.

Because in a world full of chaos,
No matter how many lifetimes pass,
I'll always search for you.

50

From time to time, I think of you,
And while the music in my headphones fades,
Thousands of smiles dance their way across my face.
As I slip into the subconscious realm of fantasy,
Emotions seal away the door to reality.

While the imaginator takes control of the mind,
Streaming the possibilities of what could be,
Soliloquies of tranquility across timelines
Are whispered from my lips as I continue to transcend
Into the heavens amongst the stars
Where you are mine and I would be yours,
Soaring through heartfelt skies over countless gardens.

I was unaware that I'd become so caught up—
That, in truth, I had been blind and oblivious,
Not noticing reality was standing at the door,
Waiting for me to let it in so things could return.

And as the music returns, the images fade,
But the feelings and desires remain standing strong,
Waiting for the next time to arrive
When I'm thinking of you.

51

Let's take it back and make everything right—
Happiness, love, and freedom amongst the stolen.
"Why take it back?" you ask with a somber face.

Because I remember the times when your smile
Alone could shine bright enough to light up heaven itself,
Perfection that never seemed to fade away
And always left me in blissful disarray.

An oblivious man once told me,
"In life, one must die before they can be free."
Well, he couldn't be more wrong, you see,
Because the heart is freedom's key.

It's been known that the eulogy of you and me
Was more than just a simple fantasy—
Chasing more than just crazy dreams,
Both wanting to simply be free.

We became strong in our own right
Where you became the light of the sun,
Lighting the world and protecting them
In the many hours of the day,
And I became the shadows of the moon,
Supporting you and watching over the world
In the silence of the night.

So let's take it back and make everything right,
And by "it," I mean the love that was stolen,
For I don't know what else to make you believe.
And after everything, how can you tell me
That you still refuse to accept and see
Maybe—just maybe—we're meant to be?

52

After a decade-long love affair,
The story finally comes to an end.
While I sit looking at the sky
Through crimson bars,
I can't help but smile,
For there you are—
Flying high, at peace,
Turning away, I think, back
To the very beginning
When light met the shadow
And when the raven fell
Deeply in love with the phoenix.

But see, we didn't know then
That, like the land and the sky,
Time divided us with day and night.
You stayed light-hearted,
Taking care of those you cared for,
Bringing joy to radiate across the land.

I stayed within the shadows,
Chained by the demons of my past—
A serial killer metaphorically,
For I shot down every relationship
To remain alone during the night watch.

I wonder sometimes if
You ever think about what could've been,
For every time, I've died inside.

53

If I were to title this chapter of my life,
I'd call it, "Unpredictable Romance and Adventure,"
For I didn't expect to find genuine potential
Nor was I prepared to connect spiritually with another.

But there you stand with that gentle smile,
Melting the ice and ringing the bells
As you danced inside the kingdom of my heart.
"What should I do?" is the question I ask myself
Because I was caught when I saw heaven in your eyes.

All I want to do is give you the world,
To grow and build an empire our souls could fly freely in,
Finding new ways to love and to be loved
And to stimulate your mind, not just your heart.

I must digress and say that before I wake into the morning sun,
I'll only see you in the world of my dreams
Where my feelings and desires can be more than a fantasy
While I admire you from afar in reality.

54

There's something in the way you smile
That creates millions of priceless moments
As it tears through the clouds,
Shining light on all the beauty of the world.

I find myself at a loss for words
Because I myself am lost in the world it creates.
I see a peaceful world full of dreams
And the finer things life can offer.

It is in these moments I never want to leave,
For the way they make me feel is irreplaceable,
So as I return to reality, I stand with the promise
To do all I can so that your smile never fades.

55

If I didn't know any better, I'd swear you were a dream.
I can't help but smile at the way your eyes light up
Or how your smile just takes my breath away,
Piercing my heart with a thousand arrows
Stolen from the great Cupid himself.

Time could continue to pass us by,
And the fire between us could grow to burn brightly
For countless years to come simply because
One can never be certain of how this story will unfold.

Most people claim to want their names in headlights
On the big screens with the baddest cars
And to live on top of the hills as fake kings and queens
Like the superstars we heard about growing up.

However, for me to be happy, I don't need all that.
What I do need is rather sweet and simple:
As I sit looking out across the starlit city,
There's always plenty of it if you're willing to give,
For I only need your love, and that will be enough.

56

I still think back to the days in high school
When you'd look my way,
And my stomach would fill with thousands of butterflies,
Each with their own emotion or reason to like you.
Now it seems surreal to think that you're mine
Or that I have the honor to make you smile every day.

It may be selfish, but I'm glad this is my dream,
For words can't describe how phenomenal you are.
So with each passing day, let each butterfly
Be a new reason you smile and a new reason I like you so.

57

Every time I gaze at the silver sparks in the sky,
I find myself thinking about you.
And in the quiet breeze, a smile subtly
Dances its way across my face,
For it seems that for every star, there
Is another reason why you're phenomenal.

If I were to trace my finger along enough of them,
I'd be able to see the smile that awakens the world
Even as you lay somewhere, resting peacefully.
It's hard to imagine that we exist under the same sky
And that the eulogy of you and me was never meant to be.

But I will enjoy the imagery of this alternate reality
As I bid you adieu, for my eyes grow weary,
And dawn approaches slowly on the horizon.
I know that under this sky, I am safe,
For in the land of dreams, I have you.

58

Here I stand before your honor and the people of the court
On trial for a crime I truly feel to be unjust,
For I am not the culprit but the victim, if you will,
Shot by the woman across from me with a bullet
That shook me to the very core of my being
As it went cleanly through my heart and pierced
The icy grip that held it prisoner for so long.

She's no criminal; in fact, she's a heroine,
For we were all smiles as she set the gun down,
Laughing as the smoke signals faded from the gun.
In the distance, we heard the wails of the approaching sirens
And knew this moment would soon come to an end.

But how can you arrest someone for something so pure?
I was reminded of the way her smile
Easily is the best part of my morning
And the greatest end to my night.

The impact from the bullet filled my heart
With millions of warm butterflies because she was near.
I had never felt happier than in those moments with her.

If you were to touch above our hearts,
You'd swear that we're the same.
And, your honor, she's intoxicated my thoughts
To where she lingers in my mind throughout the day.

Now, if this is truly a crime, then please answer me:
Why does it feel so right, and why have I never felt more alive?
It is true that she shot me in cold blood;
However, she freed me when she murdered me with love.

59

As I lay my head down, ready to dream,
My thoughts drift back to you—
The way you smile puts my soul at ease
While the gentle breeze carries the sound of your laugh
To settle the swift beat that is my heart.

Never would I have guessed that I could feel this way,
Or that someone like you could actually accept me.
It's refreshing yet frightening, to say the least,
To be accepted when most outcasted me.
Maybe for once, time will bless me with somewhere
I can finally say I belong.

Images flood my mind of the fantasies
That have yet to become reality in the eulogy
Of the epic story of you and me.
I remember a time before you when I was jaded,
Where dark skies had pleasant memories faded.

Time begins to slow; my eyes grow weary.
The thoughts begin to subside as I'm left with hope
In the idea that you may break the chains,
Setting me free to soar in the sky as I'm meant to.
As I lay my head down, ready to dream,
I think of all the possibilities of you and me.

60

With a subtle smile, I look at the clouds in the morning sky,
Thinking about the ways you were meant for me.
Is it the way your smile illuminates the evening room?
Your beauty is a pleasant sight amongst the stars.

Or could it be the way your heart is big enough for the world
But allows me to be the protector of the city within?
It took me by surprise when you became the queen
Of the bees who had worked hard to survive
In order to fill my heart with honey and not a shell.

Maybe it's the way that, when we lock eyes, I see the night sky—
Full of hopes, dreams, passion, joy, and kindness,
Making it easy to get lost in the ideal of the finer things in life.

I couldn't possibly forget the quirky personality
Or the adventurous knowledge I'm still exploring.
I think it's everything mentioned above and
What I have yet to discover.
To the phenomenal queen: I'll work to protect your heart.

61

I must hurry now, for time's almost up,
And soon, you'll be gone without knowing
The feelings and desires I have for you.

You see, when I'm out and about in the world
Or life's troubles start to get me down,
I always think of your smile to brighten my day,
And the way your hair flows gently in the breeze
Is very calming, to say the least.

With a subtle laugh, I remember the times
When love was all in the mind and chivalry
Had the respect it rightfully deserves.

There was a time when men complimented
Women simply for what they do,
Buying them flowers just because,
Never letting a day go by without showing
That, to him, she was his world.

It's that old-school love that was magical,
Extra-terrestrially spiritual, mental, and emotional.
Though I got lost in the tangent of my mind,
It's that kind of love I've dreamed of giving you,
And though it may take a while to give you
Every star in the sky with the moon, it's worth it.

Because, like finding new ways to make you smile
So that you may brighten my day,
I'd gladly dedicate my life to it.

62

Is it a crime that on the clearest of days,
I see your smiling face in the sun
As I'm taken away by the sounds of your voice
In the playful whispers in the midday breeze?

Or maybe I should ask if it is a crime
When there's a never-ending marathon
Going on in my mind and you're the only one running?
Crafting thoughts to cheer you on as you keep running for eternity
Before I'm convicted and taken away,
I must admit that everything I do, I do for you,
Counting every second until our rendezvous.

And everything I say carries the will and passion
Equal to a thousand armies within my heart.
Though once again, I must ask for clarity:
Is it a crime…that I love you so?

63

It's your smile I see
Whenever I close my eyes,
And I hear the sound of your laugh
Carried through the gentle breeze.

You radiate such life and joy—
So genuine and so pure.
Honestly, I find it refreshing.
This also marks the dawn of a new day
With the tides changing, bringing
Lots of new adventures of me and you.

There's a lot that I wish to tell you
Although it's hard to organize my thoughts
When the mind of my heart gets lost
In the world within your eyes.
Now, I ask that you be patient with me,
For soon I hope you'll come to believe
That with you is where I find my peace.

64

Often times, I think you've forgotten
How much of a treasure you truly are
Or that you don't give yourself enough credit,
And I often wish that I could give you a rose
For everything amazing about you—
There'd be enough to fill every room
In one of those mansions you see in movies.

When we first met, I couldn't help but stare.
There were a thousand ways I wanted to compliment you,
Yet none seemed to form solid, verbal thoughts.

And I must ask is it wrong that I want to know
All the things you fear,
To protect you so that you'll never be scared,
Or that I want to know all that makes you smile
So I can make it stay awhile?
And is it wrong that I want to see you shine,
Watching as all your dreams come true?

I told you in the beginning I was different,
And I guess a part of you didn't believe it.
However, I am genuine and sincere
When I say I'm invested in seeing
Your smile light the world on a daily basis.

65

When we were young, we heard stories—
Often in fairy tales—to help us sleep
And allow us to dream about being
Someone's Prince Charming or the clichéd
Knight in shining armor to a princess in distress.

I told you in the beginning I was different,
And I swear on my heart that I meant it.
I care more for your genuine emotions
Than the world's watching devotion.

I could give you the moon and the stars,
The world delivered to the palm of your hands.
All you'd have to do is simply say, "Yes."
With my heart on the line, here I stand,
Wishing to be more than just your man.

But for now, you could send me your location
So we can focus on communication
Because I wanna get to know you
And see that our feelings would be true.

66

Don't make me close one more door.
I don't want to hurt anymore.
Stay in my arms if you dare.
Must I imagine you there?

Don't walk away from me.
I'll have nothing without you.
If only you simply just knew
My feelings have always been true.

We built love in the land of dreams
Though in reality, nothing's as it seems.
You broke down all of my walls,
Knowing surely that I would fall.

You got to know a side of me
Few rarely ever get to see.
You quickly became my peace, and now
My love can't just quickly cease.

Don't imprison you and me,
Throwing away the key
So that our hearts will never be free.
And in time, you will see
That you can't run from yourself,
For there's no way to hide from your heart.

Please take my love.
I'd never ask for much—
Just all that you are
And all that you do,
So don't make me close one more door.

My heart's sinking down to the floor. I
don't want to hurt anymore.
Stay in my arms if you dare.
Must I imagine you there?

Don't walk away from me.
Please let our feelings be And
our hearts set free.
What more can I say
So that my heart can have its way?

67

What more can I do
To show you my feelings are true?
I guess I can start by saying
That I wrote this ode for you.
You see, I feel shook.

Every time I close my eyes,
My heart skips a beat at the sight of you,
And I find myself floating on emotions,
Lost in the sea of love,
And that first breath after I open my eyes
Is the best one I've ever taken,
For there you are in front of me,
And my dream turns out to be reality.

I've been ready to give you the world
In spite of my own insecurities.
I'd have brought down the heavens
If I thought it would please you.
You are my best friend,
And without you I'd be a fool.

You are my greatest strength
And also my biggest weakness,
For I'd die before I let harm come to you.
Now, I don't mean that to overwhelm you,
But I've come to see
That a life without you is not one I want.

For my storm is a movement by myself,
But with you, it's a real force.
So don't be afraid to fall in love
Because with me, your dreams will come true
As mine do every day with you.

68

I think of you in the early morning light.
Your beauty and love are well worth the fight.
It's so easy to get lost in your eyes,
Watching the story your heart cries.
I let my mind drift into a small daydream.

I asked you to dance, and you replied with a smile,
Hinting that you'd consider staying awhile.
We laughed and spun to Love's slow jam
While I whispered to you all that I am.
You said, "Forever is a long song away."
In kind, I replied, "Don't go; just let the record play."

And maybe it's my own intuition about your last mistake,
But I'm serving as an intervention for your heartbreak.
I also know that you're highly educated
And slightly sophisticated, so this talk
May all seem a tad overrated.

The record jumps, pulling us from the moment,
Which means reality is pulling me back.
Before I leave, I wish to make this statement:
I am not like the guys who hurt you in the past,
And if all goes well, I'd hope to be your last.

69

We've come so far,
And yet we've so far to go.
We see in the distance
Our long way home.
My heart was always yours to have.
Yours was always mine.
We'll love each other in and out of time.

When the first ray of light broke across the ocean
And the first tree struggled from the forest floor,
I have always loved you more.
You freed your soul,
Gave your caution to the breeze
Just to put your mind at ease.

I see you when I close my eyes,
Telling me my heart is wise.
You are my strength.
So of course, when my heart drums,
I'll be the first to fight
Even if you're not always right.

You intoxicate my thoughts with wine.
And from the butterflies in my chest,
I knew I had to make you mine.
With you, my love will fly
Peacefully, like birds in the sky.

You are my best, truest friend.
Without you, my world surely would end.
I know I've asked this all the time,
But could we please dance one more time?

With promise and vows of forever,
I knew I'd be the luckiest man ever.
I look to you to brighten my day,
And with a smile, all my stress melts away.
Mmmm…God, how I love your smile.

You've seen me pummeled by circumstance.
Lost, wounded, broken by chance.
I cried to the heavens—desperately cried—
To turn our nightmares into dreams.

We've come so far,
And yet we've so far to go.
We see in the distance
Our long way home.

My heart was always yours to have,
And yours was always mine.
We'll love each other in and out,
In and out,
In and out
…Of time.

Made in the USA
Middletown, DE
08 July 2024